EVEN SO

First published in 2008 by
The Dedalus Press
13 Moyclare Road
Baldoyle
Dublin 13
Ireland

www.dedaluspress.com

Editor: Pat Boran

ISBN 978 1 904556 99 2 (paper)
ISBN 978 1 906614 01 0 (bound)

Dedalus Press titles are represented in North America
by Syracuse University Press, Inc., 621 Skytop Road,
Suite 110, Syracuse, New York 13244, and in the UK by
Central Books, 99 Wallis Road, London E9 5LN.

Cover image © Tim Guthrie

The Dedalus Press receives financial assistance from
An Chomhairle Ealaíon / The Arts Council, Ireland

Even So

New & Selected Poems

Mark Roper

DEDALUS PRESS
DUBLIN, IRELAND

ACKNOWLEDGEMENTS

As well as previously uncollected poems, *Even So* includes work from the following collections: *The Hen Ark* (1990), co-published by Peterloo Poets and Salmon Poetry; *Catching The Light* (1996), co-published by Peterloo Poets and Lagan Press; *The Home Fire* (1998), published by Abbey Press; and *Whereabouts* (2005), co-published by Peterloo Poets and Abbey Press.

My sincere thanks, for all their support and encouragement, are due to Harry Chambers of Peterloo Poets; Jessie Lendennie of Salmon Poetry; Pat Ramsey of Lagan Press, and Adrian Rice of Abbey Press.

Acknowledgements and thanks are due to the editors of the following, in which some of the new poems in this volume first appeared: *New Hibernian Review, The North, Poetry Ireland Review, Revival, The SHOp, Best of Irish Poetry 2009* and *University of Reading Creative Arts Anthology 2008*.

Thanks also to the staff at The Tyrone Guthrie Centre at Annaghmakerrig, and The Blue Mountain Centre in Upstate New York.

For Roz Cowman and Edward Reid Power

Contents

Introduction by Carol Rumens / 11

New Poems

You / 17
Cut / 18
Snow / 19
Hummingbird / 20
Out of Water / 22
Barn Owl / 23
The Crossing / 24
After the Holiday / 25
Mine / 26
Aberdevine / 27
Goldcrest / 28
Sun / 29
Someone Else / 31
Path / 32
Cattle / 33
The Gift of Tongues / 35
Manet's 'The Fifer' / 36
The Mixed Message / 37
Cry / 38
Limbo / 39
Deer / 40
Throat / 41
Reach / 42
The Case / 43
The Blazer / 45
Brent Geese / 46
Dolphins / 47

Small / 48
In Praise of Pottering / 49
A Day / 50
The Class / 52
Evening / 53
Voice / 54
Four Birds / 55
The Sea Lion / 56
Ghost / 57
Colonoscope / 58
Golden Verse / 59
House Martins / 60
Storks / 61
Still Life / 62
Even So / 63

from *The Hen Ark (1990)*

Cleaning Ladies / 67
Ann Jackson / 68
A Woman of Anglo-Ireland / 70
Soft Day / 71
Easter in Firle Park / 72
Father / 73
Yellow and Blue / 74
Harvest / 76
Soap / 78
Firelight / 80
In the Choir Stall / 82
The Coroner / 83
Hair Piece / 85
The Hen Ark / 86

from *Catching the Light* (1996)

Angel / 89
The Last Tiger in Piltown / 91
Wood / 93
North Coast / 94
Edgeways / 95
The Census / 96
You / 97
The Silence Cloth / 99
Here / 101
Breaking Ground / 102
Main de Gloire / 103
Palm / 104
Red-Handed / 105
Herons / 106
Halcyon / 108
November / 109
Marsh Marigolds / 110
Appetite / 111
No Problem / 112
The Sun Room / 114
Letter from Ladakh / 115
Catching the Light / 117
Unbecoming / 119
Prayer / 120
What The Deer Said / 121
Scythe / 122

from *Whereabouts* (2005)

Swallow / 127
Him / 128
Woodpecker / 129
Skip / 130
The Toy Museum / 131

Home / 132
And This is True / 133
Sleeping with the Kingfisher / 135
The Inner Poet / 136
The First Move / 138
Digestion / 139
Red Admirals / 140
Entries / 141
The Home Fire / 142
Saturday Morning / 144
For All You Know / 146
Starling / 147
Leaf / 148
Face / 149
Rain / 150
Need / 151
Career / 152
The Broken Fields / 154
Van Gogh's 'The Farm' / 155
Peck / 156
The Robin / 157
Swan House / 159
Magwitch / 160
Snipe / 161
Elder / 162
Harriers / 163
Heron / 164
Whereabouts / 165

Introduction

To write poetry about the natural world today is a very different enterprise from that of the nineteenth century. Celebration and wonder are not prohibited, and perhaps are more necessary than ever, but the writer now requires a sharper, humbler sense of ecological responsibility, and an intellectual grasp that comes closer to that of the scientist, perhaps. Mark Roper's poems are exemplary, gathering their meticulous observations into an unobtrusive lyric or narrative focus without being tempted to impose an insistent poetic ego, or "to degrade a mystery into a problem".* If nature is no longer elevated to a great, god-like teacher of humanistic ideals, it is still perceived as numinous and tutelary. But the approach to its mystery is always through attention to the physical revelation, recorded in fluent, vivid, almost offhanded descriptive strokes—and well-judged silence.

Nature poetry, unlike landscape painting, must avoid seeming static. Roper has a particular gift for revealing movement and process—whether it is the faint shift of falling leaves, the meandering approach of cattle, casually fascinated by their human observer, or the flight of birds. "Starlings join to make one single-minded machine./ Whatever tree they land on/ becomes a starling tree." Storks, "lifted and added to themselves", are transformed into "one bird made/ of hundreds of birds, one great drift/ which would not seem to move a muscle/ but alters all the while its every angle". The perspective is not always that of the human observer. The sparrowhawk is "the wood's worst shadow/ the one which suddenly/ replaces your own". Watching a live goldfish being devoured by four black beetles, the speaker feels the jaws working at his own flesh long after he has intervened and "killed them all". Struggling, bloodstained nature requires not moral condemnation but asks the

---

* William Walsh, *The Use of Imagination*, p.64.

poet to enter skins other than his own, and to understand that he, too, is subject to the processes of destruction: "What's the great sun in all its glory/ but a lustrous hen, pecking us, itself, away?" ('Peck').

Informed, possibly, by the Zen practice of listening with the eyes and looking out through the ears, Roper evokes a range of sound effects, sometimes onomatopoeic, sometimes mysteriously visual. There are the brent geese with their "grumbled calls" , the goldcrest's "thin pheet-pheet in a conifer", the "blackbird's slither/ and scald,/ a wren's rattle". But often the human senses seem to coalesce: "All over the sky/ these scars of sound,/ this listening." ('Snipe')

This is nature de-romanticised, where birds sometimes move like machinery, preying on other creatures, even their own kind, and producing sounds that are not always evocative of human emotions, and do not encode messages of the divine. Even the "terrible" call of Roper's totemic bird, the heron, conveys "utter lack of meaning and hope". On the other hand, an encounter often occurs, and uncaged wings disturb or even enclose the speaker's world. In 'Entries', a kind of triangular love-poem, a couple have been observing swifts, "until they flew inside us," and the birds, or the memory of them, will in turn be entered "by the light of our watching them together". Sometimes, confused, the bird invades human space, like the goldcrest who flies into a glass door, drops stunned at the poet's feet, and then abruptly, beautifully, recovers, and takes off as if nothing had happened. These moments of connection seem close to the poet's heart, unleashing his careful excitement, his sense of privilege.

No bird is sentimentally elevated, but none is entirely earth-bound, either, as we see in this marvellous little portrait of a swallow:

A spent firework
on the lawn.

Tiny feet still
hooked on space.

Wings wind-sleek,
head sleek with wind.

So full of flight
it must have died

of ripeness.
In the tail's V

a stalk of sky.

Though a favourite subject for many contemporary poets, few
have written about wild birds with this degree of tenderness and
panache. But Roper's bird-poems are part of a bigger picture of
response to the fascination of lives not-fully-approachable. There are
love poems, poems about children and parents and childlessness: we
see a bevy of cleaning ladies "who like a bit of sauce/ who make ends
meet/ who go without saying", and meet 'The Last Tiger in Piltown',
a strange and lonely beast, part human, part media invention,
perhaps. Another new attribute for the nature poem is a sense of
humour. But in 'Prayer' it is the wounded human animal that is
given a voice, a multitude of abused children whose dangerously
insistent apostrophe echoes Paul Celan's 'Tenebrae':

Look at us, Lord, praise us,
real tonight as each other,
as real as can be. Beyond belief
our beauty, our right to be here.

Like another of his mentors, Edward Thomas, Roper is blest
with a mournful-happy receptivity to the beauty of rain. However,
the rain that falls all day in 'The Mixed Message' is not only
wrapping the world in a gentle "grey blanket" but defiling it: "All
day the waterlily fouled, / the sugar maple undone."

Despite such sharp reminders of our failure to be good
custodians of the earth, Roper's warnings mostly come wrapped in
the subtle shapes of observation and empathy, and a diction that
flattens the rhetoric of simplistic binary oppositions. In 'And This is
True', for example, there is a double 'turn'. Having shown us the fox
at ease and in its element, he reverses the image to show the fox

injured, fearful of humankind. This is also true, the poem admits, but once again the vision 'turns', the speaker re-discovers the fox happily ambling towards him, as in the beginning, "through campion, / bluebell, ramson, on a spring evening", and exhorts the reader severely, "Do not doubt it".

In the earlier work there is a fruitful tension between the poetic demand of "Keeping the wide world wide" ('Barn Owl'), and narrowing it down "until there is only what there is" ('Scythe'). The more recently written title-poem seems to settle for "what there is" and suggests how the quietest narrative may re-thread the disconnected:

> Nettles by the wall, where the cattle cannot reach.
> Broken, silvered stalks of cow-parsley. A strand
> of barbed wire, rusted, drooping from pale posts.

Even So reveals the extent to which Mark Roper's move from the UK to the Kilkenny countryside in 1980 has liberated his imagination and, by allowing him to report on lived, day-to-day experience, helped him to become an extraordinarily distinguished 'nature poet'—or, perhaps the better term, 'poetic naturalist'. Ireland's gift to the poet has been an environment that is still relatively unspoiled, and continues to permit ancient harmonious relationships between land-working humans and the birds, beasts, woodland, pools and pastures with which their lives interweave. Roper's gift to his adopted home, and to the great poetic tradition of 'nature writing' in these islands, is laid out here, in this wonderfully varied miscellany of new work and selections from his earlier volumes. Despite the poet's realism, it is surely not inappropriate if the book's title faintly reminds us of the poem 'The Oxen' in which, writing in the terrible year of 1915, Thomas Hardy recalls the childhood legend of the cattle who kneel down on Christmas Eve, still "hoping it might be so".

—Carol Rumens

New Poems

You

Under all our furniture,
our cushions and our carpets,
you are always listening.

From the corner of an eye,
in paint behind a mirror,
we sense your attention.

A window seems suddenly
to reflect another world. You
are not who we think you are.

In the dusty air of a room
we'll never find, your tapes turn.
How should we talk before you?

Last thing at night, in silence
deepened by a fridge-hum's halt,
you catch our breath. You have

no words to describe yourself.
Darkness under a lifted board.
Creaks as we try to sleep.

You'll never be done with us.

Cut

So you drive to work
thinking of this and that
and suddenly find
you don't know
what road you're on
you've never seen
these hedges before
you look in the mirror
and there's that garden
those iris leaves
which cut so clean
you don't feel a thing
until minutes later
your skin parts
and the blood wells
from a cut as clean as that
of Saladin's sword
on which a handkerchief
might fall and
continue to fall
in two halves still
thinking they're one

Snow

Even though it's dark when you wake,
you know it has snowed. A chill silence
under the curtain. Cold glow on the wall.

And when you get up, on the sill you find
its perfect lid. You open the window
and touch. It takes and holds your hand.

Later you can run out the front door,
throw yourself on its mercy. But soon
you'll be back indoors, soaked and frozen.

Better to wrap up warm, spend the day reading.
Barbed wires of birdtrack. White branches
underlined in black. Cars asleep under ermine.

Soon the roads will open, their gutters run
with mush. Best to keep going, out to the edge
of town and on into snowquietened fields.

Here you can catch a missel thrush in the act
of burgling a hawthorn, watch it gobble rubies.
A bullfinch's rose coat, a blackbird's gold beak,

shine as if fresh-minted. Your own footprints
follow you wherever you go. And it's best
to keep going, through mauve and indigo shadow,

your own colours deepening, hardening into you.

Hummingbird

Not just how
it hung so still
in the quick of its wings,
all gem and temper
anchored in air;

not just the way
it moved from shelf
to shelf of air,
up down, here there,
without moving;

not just how it flicked
its tongue's thread
through each butter-yellow
foxglove flower
for its fix of sugar;

not just the vest's
electric emerald,
the scarf's scarlet,
not just the fury
of its berry-sized heart,

but also how the bird
would soon be found
in a tree nearby,
quiet as moss at the end
of a bare branch,

wings closed around
its sweetening being,
and then how light
might touch its throat
and make it glow,

as if it were the tip
of a cigarette
smouldering
on the lip of a world,
whose face,

in the lake's hush
and the stir of leaves,
might appear,
for a moment,
composed.

Out of Water

Rain nags and needles the pond
but whatever it writes is erased.

At last it loses heart but leaves
a green light over lily-pads

into which a grey wagtail struts,
bent on one thousand prostrations.

Water won't take the repeated
impression of the bird's lemon breast.

No ice is cut by the pond-skater,
no oarprint left by the boatman.

One by one raindrops slide from
a leaf and are never seen again.

Sun lifts his fist and hammers
at the pond's door. No reply.

Water wrinkles its brow, as if
something had slipped its mind.

Barn Owl

Still there, crossing Cahill's Hill last thing.
Spirit-lamp we feared extinguished here.
Nightlight, heightening the silence.

Still there, knowing what you know.
Heading out over the fields, sinking back
into a black still deep enough to hold you.

Farming the dark. Polishing things off.
Keeping the wide world wide a while.

The Crossing

One day you will walk down a road
you've walked down a thousand times.

Down through trees where water
burns in the sumps and gutters.

On the tarmac a lattice of shadow.
On the high wires lines of light.

And the words will be taken
clean out of your mouth.

And there'll be nothing for it—
you will not live to tell the tale.

How close they will come,
the birch twig, the silence inside a sloe.

How you will wonder
what you ever did before.

After the Holiday

After the holiday
we drive home, check the house,
walk into the garden.

After the dark red desert,
after all those animals and birds,
I feared it might disappoint.

After all the bright talk
with our friends, I feared
we might be lonely.

We listen to the stream,
its two notes. A robin
taps out its take on things.

The apples are ripening.
The wild ginger's in flower.
Slowly the known air

begins to unclothe us.
Across the field the horses
make their shy approach,

like our lives, coming back.

Mine

He was mine, the first adult thing I'd owned. Mine, and not my sister's. He sat on a table by my bed, the last thing I saw at night. As I fell asleep, I'd watch him ride through the traffic, down the Great North Road, under the railway bridge, past the Odeon into Greenhill.

He was made of ivory, a brave on a rearing stallion, clutching for a spear a scant wire. Not new. The feather had gone from his head. The baize on the oblong base was torn.

If I were to come across him now, at the back of some cupboard, buried in some trunk, if I were to try to lift him out, I would feel not just my own small hands but all the hands, refusing to let go; all the voices crying *Mine*.

Aberdevine

At the feeder after weeks away.
Breast from this angle acid-yellow.
Belly paler. Crown black.

Smaller than a greenfinch, brighter.
Back and cheeks more vivid green.
But finch-beaked.

Wings black, barred with yellow.
Black tail sided yellow.
Siskin, says the book.

As far as the eye can see,
as the tongue can tell,
a *siskin,* a name

which the bird has found
a better fit than *aberdevine*—
M.18. Origin unknown.

*Little real currency. Now rare
or obsolete.* A name lost
for a partner. Its own lament.

Goldcrest

Fair enough its thin pheet-pheet in a conifer;
fair enough a glimpse of yellow crest.
But this one flew straight into this glass door
and dropped on this metal balcony at my feet,
and though I could tell it was still breathing
it had hit the glass so hard it seemed
I would just have to sit and watch it die.
I could admire the rust and buttercup cap;
the surprisingly long feathered feet. Gusts
ruffled the mud-green coat, showing grey inside.
I kept looking away, then I'd touch it
with a pencil, just to check it was breathing.
I know how inspiration comes like a bird
but this one was real, stunned, awry
on the flaking sludge-blue paint. How did it
make that mistake, not see itself coming?
Were others watching? Was it being missed?
The more I looked, the less I knew.
I turned it around, in case it woke and flew
into the glass again. Then it flew away.
No slow coming-to. It just flew, as if
it had never stopped. Vanished. Got on
with its business. So I got on with mine.

Sun

It was May. Sun was dripping down
on the sea, on the cliffs, on the field
full of horses and foals.

Sun had melted the top of the sea
to drifts of metal, a shift of glitters,
seeps of purple

all slightly asway, deeply moved,
cut and puffed with white, circled
by a light horizon.

In the cliffs sun picked out rose
and loden, soaked mauves and inky washes,
slithers of quartz.

It sharpened the scent of gorse, seaweed's
iodine, the rotting musk of hawthorn,
elder's pissy tang.

Tucked in their hollows, campion and bluebell,
stitchwort, orchid, foxglove
all looked up to it.

Gulls cried, horses cropped, small birds nattered.
There was a distant murmur of waves,
there was total silence.

The horses and foals, many-coloured,
lay and walked on sheets of daisies.
The sun held them all.

It leant on the broad back of the sea,
on the small faces of the flowers,
on the ancient rocks.

It leant on the white foal, her hip
buckled, on the stillness around her,
her baffled gaze.

It concentrated on nothing in particular,
fell with an even hand, would do so all day,
long into the evening.

Someone Else

How the eye lies when it surveys the scene—
a shadow on the ground, cloud across a mountain,
a star in the sky—as if these things were connected,
as if they knew about each other's existence.

What a frame-up, what a stitch-up eye contrives,
and just so tongue adds one thing to another
as if they followed on, as if it all made sense
and only remained to be put into words.

But where can you put one word if not after another?
And who were you ever talking to anyway
if not a phantom, a projection, if not
yourself, your parents, if not anyone

but the one who stands there in front of you,
who lies there beside you, pretending to listen,
pretending to understand, all the while
lost in the immensities of her own thought?

Path

The front garden, snug in houselight.
A black wooden gate. Blue shadows.
Shrubs drooping over the short concrete path
leading to our door. I look down on it
each night, last thing: an outdoor room,
cut in half by an empty path.

On either side the flowers, the hedge,
the roads, fields, rivers, mountains, sea.
The path a line drawn between them,
as if to break their spell. It seems
nothing could cross that line,
no harm ever come down it—

though it lies quite open to what
will come, the morning, the gifts,
the ghosts, the hawk-headed gods.

Cattle

Up through the bowl of the evening
the cattle come in ones and twos
to where I stand at a red gate,
staring into space, not calling these cattle

who come anyway, slow and vague
at first, picking at tufts of grass,
heads and udders heavy,
coats a fresh white and black

in the half-light. Up they come
to stand in a row and stare at me,
their eyes waterbrown overlaid
with blurred and smoky blue,

their gaze modest, grave, sad.
Skin around mouths hard and moist,
grey patching a clean pink.
Odd bristles lifting, turning to light.

Black numbers stand out clearly
on yellow ear-tags. A tongue reaches
for the cold iron of the gate.
Their bodies are all touching.

Behind the row of heavy skulls,
the heavier skulls of the hills.
Fields hung like patchwork.
A thin stitching of hedge.

We stare at each other. Our breath
comes and goes, into our bodies,
back to the world, into our bodies,
back to the world, as if there were

nothing more to say, though of course
there is, always, as one cow turns
to lick a flank, one bends to eat,
slowly the rest start to wander off.

The Gift of Tongues

All year round rooks call
from trees, fields, air,
a monotonous chant,
a bleak satisfaction,
self-possessed as stone.

In Spring things change.
Burps and gurgles
interrupt the broadcast.
Hiccups and belches
bubble up throats.

A new, gooey language
strains from beaks
gummed with frogspawn,
with yolk, with sticky bud,
marsh marigold, mud.

Manet's 'The Fifer'

He will never be heard,
the music is long gone.

He stands there alone,
surrounded by silence.

Feet at the right angle.
His poor arms aching.

His breath forever
taken and held.

You'd like to touch him,
take the fife from his hands.

But you cannot touch him.

The Mixed Message

All day rain, steady and plentiful,
blessing the hills, the leaves, the lichen.

All day its sound around the house,
as if someone held us, loved us.

All day wrapped in its grey blanket,
homesick inside its lullaby.

All day the world licking its skin,
washing its face like a cat.

All day the endless coins of rain
dropping into the bowl of earth.

All day the grateful trees,
their wholly open hands.

All day the plane over the lakes,
collecting the samples, the evidence.

All day the build-up in the soil,
the poison added to everything.

All day the waterlily fouled,
the sugar maple undone.

All day eating ourselves
out of house and home.

All day the mixed message,
the ruin in the rain.

Cry

If there were listeners out there,
and if, having found us, they were
to tune in, what would they pick up,
what would be the sound to reach?

A sound perhaps which has risen
from the earth's changing face
unchanged—the call, say, of a loon,
the same over millions of years.

That cry of bereft belonging.
That forlorn, water-thrilled psalm.

*So that was what it was like to live
in that once green, that once blue world.*

And they would train their instruments elsewhere.

Limbo

I found them when a wind
blew our bird-box down.

They must have been there
for months, bunched up,

beaks still raised and open.
The nest had cushioned their fall.

They were coloured shadows,
half eaten away, but their colours,

painted on what was almost air,
were all present and correct—

as if the chicks clung to the belief
there was something to live up to,

someone to deliver them.

Deer

How long had I been standing among them
on the lawn in the darkness and had they
slowly surrounded me or had I walked
unwittingly between them and how could they
have been so invisible so quiet
and would I ever have known there had been
anything there at all had not the air
begun it seemed to crumble open
break apart push past me pick up speed
and stream and rush away into the wood—
I saw nothing I did not know what was there
nor what was gone I was left standing
in thin air in an absence into which
a word began to fall but could not rise
to this sudden emptying of a space
I had not known had not known was filled.

Throat

Through the swimmers and standers,
the lilos and pedalos,
the ball throwers and catchers,
the canoes and rowing boats;
through noon glitter and noise
on the brown, crowded lake comes
a shiver and shockwave of swallows,
a blueblack dazzle of blades
which could open our throats
and be up and over the hills
before we'd time to notice
our breath had been taken away

Reach

Out of the dark a hand reaches
for a glass ashtray, which holds
a pipe, a cleaning tool, spills
coloured red, green, yellow.

A piece of tobacco taken from
a brown wallet is torn, shredded,
pushed and prodded into the pipe,
its rim charred, stem bitten down.

A spill is dipped into the fire.
The small flame brought to the pipe
runs and dances over the bowl,
and your face, lit for a second,

disappears in a puff of smoke.

The Case

Seen from the plane, fields,
through a skim of cloud,
seem to form a chessboard;

irregular squares,
buff or muddied green,
hedged in by hedge;

two or three in shape
and colour vaguer, where
one might perhaps slip

away from the game;
where I might perhaps
come across you again,

by a sump of water
slick with grass blades
under hawthorn trees,

whose each leaf
wears a ring of rain;
the rainwater the colour

of that cigarette case,
made of aluminium
from a crashed warplane,

its hinge out of true
and the catch broken,
the brown elastic slack;

on the lid, graved
with a brad or cut
with a burin, a pattern

perhaps, perhaps a maze,
to the heart of which
I'm still making my way,

unless I have got there,
and am still trying
to make my escape.

The Blazer

Still bright, the black, white and red stripes,
the brass buttons. Only the sleeve ends
have begun to decay, looking singed,
as if the garment were very slowly burning.

Your hockey colours, from R. Buttress & Co.
Crossed sticks and the college initials.
Still wearable, though no one would now.
You wore it on special summer days.

It still holds your odour. My hands still
hesitate to enter the long pockets.
Once you'd have found me down there,
loose change, fresh-faced, an unfinished sum.

Only you knew how much I was worth.
Only you could say how I should be spent.

Brent Geese

Raggedly gathered on the edge
of a swell, unwieldy, graceless,

how much they seem at home,
jostling, dibbling, squabbling.

What it's like in those ranks
of dipped livery, sky-relinquished,

settling down, how they knew
where to land, you don't know.

What is it in you answers
to their grumbled calls?

On the little shore of what you know,
you stand. You stand by these geese.

Of their endless wobble and sway
in the sea's bash and shifting glitter,

you are part, your not knowing is part.

Dolphins

They slip through the surface below the cliff,
two adults and a child,
rolling and folding their longed-for lengths.

We watch with two minds
this vision of fin
framed in all we now think of as loss.

Already they seem belated, shadows
of former selves,
apparitions rising from ruin.

Foam flares from their breaking backs
like words erased
as soon as they're uttered.

They rise and fall, as if trying
to mend the water.
The sea, in their wake, appears to heal.

Small

You wouldn't work for the police,
guide the blind, fetch a pair of slippers.
Unlike a dog. And, unlike a dog,
who needs to be taken, you took yourself
for walks. But, when it came to food,
you liked to be led to your bowl.
From early afternoon until five,
the appointed hour, you'd sit and wait
at the open kitchen door. You needed
someone to walk beside, to lean against.
This was part of eating: how first we'd cross
the floor then reach the bowl together.
You'd bow your head, eat and look up,
what might have been trust
in the soft wet of your eyes.
Even when you could no longer swallow
you still liked to be led that way.
You'd lick at the juice, from all
the different flavoured foods we tried,
and look up: puzzle now in that trust.
So, when we took you to the vet,
you came out of the basket, ears pricked,
waiting to be led to the bowl.
One last walk across the floor together.
One last look: your eyes, like pebbles
lifted from clear water, fading.

In Praise of Pottering

Let us not try to seize the moment.
Rather let us rearrange the shed,
put the red flowerpots all in one pile,
the black in another, as we did last year.

Rather than decide we must change diet,
let's drink too much coffee, eat too much cheese.
As for exercise, let us take it as and when
we want, not because we ought.

The improvement of each shining hour?
Let them go by as if inexhaustible.
Marvel how we manage not to trouble them.
There are stars whose light has not reached us yet.

In the Sunflower Nebula each gaseous head
of each cometary knot is twice our solar system's size.
Very little happens for a clear reason.
It is not our fault we grow old and die.

A Day

as high and old,
as empty and still
as a cathedral

*

whose all
it takes a leaf
to loosen, drift,
twist, touch
down, settle

*

where air
is a deer
at the edge
of a clearing,
on the brink
of speech

*

which folds into
its deepest reaches
a pheasant's
wounded tune

*

where sycamore
without a sound
slips its dress
to the ground

*

which tastes of
must, mould,
mycelium, mire

*

where the lake is
a mirror in which
nothing happens
again and again

The Class

Peeling lemon walls. Pencil shavings.
On the whiteboard strange equations.

Out the window the odd pigeon,
a small town's scruffy, cluttered grace.

Years now, in the room at the top
of the house, we've tried to make amends.

Bringing to the class our gentle evidence.
The cases we have tried to construct.

It's not about conviction, we know.
We know justice can never be done.

The innocent and the guilty,
we try to make them sing.

More and more we go by the sound of it.
The best bits we learn to make up.

Evening

blue shadow in a wood
a whisper of finches
the light failing

a grass-choked path
willowherb seeding
ragwort and bramble

black and silver water
after-circles of fish
uneasy reeds

a crow hung from a tree
stalks on a dungheap
a rake a rusty spade

up ahead a house
a few flowers
the scent of smoke

an arm in a window
a woman making bread
and you yourself

in there sitting down
to eat unable to take
any of it in

Voice

That voice I can hear in the room—
can I be certain it's mine?
When you ask me how I'm feeling,
who is it replies I'm fine?

I would like to say I love you
but the words stick in my throat.
I was always too scared to sing
in case I hit the wrong note.

You say there's no need to worry,
this is groundless fear.
I talk to myself in the mirror,
in both of my eyes a tear.

A short prayer penetrates heaven
but I've not spoken all day.
I'm down on my knees and thinking,
I can't think of a thing to say.

I tell you it's time we split up.
This is it, farewell, goodbye.
You hold me firm in your arms.
Everything I say is a lie.

Four Birds

WOOD PIGEON

clatters from canopy,
claps its wings, mounts
a staircase of air,
reaches a landing
and lets itself drop,
crosses the sky so,
up hill, down dale

KINGFISHER

that rapid dash
across the lake
enough to light
its turquoise lamp

KESTREL

drifts across plateaus
of air, comes to a cliff, dis-
tils to a drop, spills.

SPARROWHAWK

the wood's worst shadow
the one which suddenly
replaces your own.

The Sea Lion

In the eyes of an old sea lion
which has buried itself in sand high up a beach,
to be left alone to die,
you meet your own reflection.

Does it see how nothing ends or begins,
does it see how empty the beach becomes
when the birds lift and the wind drops
and the light presses down? Does it see

the beach where it was born, each wave?
Do the unjoined rib and broken shell
scattered over the sand make it feel
something must hold everything together,

or does it, at the end, feel nothing,
no desire to remain, none to leave?
Does it see its life now as a rock
to which it knows it can't return,

is the wind all it feels, are wind and rock
about to become what they were before
these eyes were? These eyes into which
sand has already begun to drift.

Ghost

It wasn't a ghost, knocking at the window. Not, after all, a ghostly hand, only a frog, jumping up from the deep hole it had fallen into, trying to escape but only able to reach the bottom of this half-underground window.

It had made a sound like a knock. And the frog did look like a hand in the air, its white belly, its front legs stretched up like a thick finger.

But of course it wasn't trying to attract my attention, knocking so insistently. It couldn't have seen me here. Couldn't have known I'd open the window, catch it in my hand, take it through the room to the small pool outside.

I shouldn't even mention it. A coil of energy, leaf-green, which seemed to be letting itself be carried—as if it had to go this way, as if we were crossing a path laid down deep in the world.

That small bundle of bones in my hand's bundle of bones. The splash as it entered the water. The sound of my feet on the gravel.

Colonoscope

The tiny camera travels
down memory lane.

Finds, in the folds of my colon,
the hands of my fathers,

painted so long ago
on the walls of the cave.

The ancestral grip,
the hold they have on me.

The blueprint my body
is primed to follow.

Finds, in the cell's obedience,
the son's obedience.

Golden Verse

The calf had wandered into a poem,
drawn to the sweet hay of chosen words.

Her sharp hooves, her tongue's rough river
could take nothing from that spoil of gold.

Her long, soft ears, her sad eyes, opened wide:
she thought she heard, deep inside those stalks,

her mother, and her mother's mother,
and her mother's mother's mother.

She thought she could see, littering roots,
scraps of leather, flecks of yellowed bone.

House Martins

we start like rain start like rain
one or two then one and two

then everywhere for hours air
round with us with us and ours

our scrawl of smalt and stringing inks
our skift and skirr and skreel

the heat and seethe and stink of us
a bound noun all speed and wheel

Storks

They come in over the water like smoke,
            long horizontals of vague crayon,
a shifting sentence whose sense and shape
            is subject to constant correction.

From their rickety homes high on poles,
            from villages all over the place
they've been lifted and added to themselves
            and spiralled high into sky above sea.

Now they are one bird, one bird made
            of hundreds of birds, one great drift
which would not seem to move a muscle
            but alters all the while its every angle.

Across to this peninsula they shift and spread
            and the bird made of all the birds
fills the air, rises and falls, a mix of sticks,
            a fluent roof, a scattered floating thatch,

and a wing made out of many birds
            (though never out of the same birds)
is opened out and stretched towards the ground.
            There is something here they need to ascertain

and when you happen to glance out over the sea
            the bird made of all birds, though right here,
is also spread out far into the distance,
            drawn as if by an easy breath west.

Still Life

As mist burns from its mirror
the lake is entered by birch and pine.

A heron locks onto its shadow.
Ripple shivers reed and alder.

The lake has dusted its face
with a glitter of insect husk

and the sequin I swim out towards
is a fish, half its face torn off:

a stitch, not a snag, in the scene.

Even So

Six cows in a row against a low stone wall.
Behind, at an angle, running away into distance,
another stone wall, ten tall beech trees spaced along it.

The cows lined up as if to watch me pass.
Patience of their hefty, long-suffering heads.
Gentle riverlight of their eyes.

Coats the colour of what, exactly? I cannot quite say.
A dark brown earth. Clay stained with iron.
Rough coats, weather-worsened, stuck with mud and twig.

Sky an empty November blue. The beech trunks
gunmetal grey, the beech leaves mustard and ginger,
the colour of the cows, but more faded and more bright.

Sadness that comes with autumn. The fieldstones
locked into their leaning, flowered with lichen.
The wall's gappy jigsaw. Its leap and bound.

No matter how hard I look, I cannot see through it.
A few beech leaves on the grass, the flat light
caught in their curls. Their spines pencil-grey.

Nettles by the wall, where the cattle cannot reach.
Broken, silvered stalks of cow-parsley. A strand
of barbed wire, rusted, drooping from pale posts.

from *The Hen Ark* (1990)

Cleaning Ladies

Through the cloisters of the academy
go the round women
brides of the broom
sisters of sweeping

who wait at the pithead
who wait at the docks
who wait by the phone

whose reward is bingo
whose reward is cancer
whose reward is the church

pillars of society
fillers of vacuum
psalters of earth

through the groves of academia
go the golden girls
bluebells of smoke
in their lungs

who like a bit of sauce
who make ends meet
who go without saying

Ann Jackson

"Ann Jackson, born in the City of
Waterford of English parents, had several
horns growing upon her body."
— *Waterford*, Charles Smith (1745)

Her sour breath
reaches down the years
like a wasp
busying through leaves.

*'She had not the evacuation
proper to her sex.'*
Bureaucracy of blood
sealed off frontiers,

pikestaffed her skin,
shut her up
in a cupboard of bark.

*'She spoke but little
and that not plainly.'*

What dark tides broke
against the soft lever
of her tongue?

What vixen prowl
obeyed the curfew
of her steepled hide?

*'Her eyes looked
very dead.'*

Did her mind ride free
on a golden wind
above that pelt of dross?

Maculate conception,
hornchild, scapegrace,

I wish her a fair hearing,
an absence of mirrors,
erosion.

A Woman of Anglo-Ireland

My husband left me without a word,
without a penny. To raise our daughter
I worked nights in a bar, high and dry
in a welter of loosened tongues.

We lived by the river. Its lights
furnished our home. At summer's end
we gathered teazles and made them
into toys for sale in town.

I thought we were happy
but she left when she reached sixteen.
I fastened the boreen leaves behind her,
let the river be my only road.

It brings me wood, fattens mussels,
removes my small leavings. I love
its moist kiss in my lungs,
its silver hands between my legs.

You might think I can't cope.
Briars fillet the roof, books rot,
grease thickens, nothing works.

But I stood on the shore with four
dog foxes in a cathedral of moonlight
and they were not afraid of me.

Soft Day

My feet leave no print.
Nothing autographs the air.

Horses plough mist. Looms
of gorse spin scant curtains.

Time stands still. History
happens elsewhere. A noise

in a room of cloud might be
a name lost forever.

Green skin conceals a labyrinth
of water. I trust nothing.

I learn a moorhen's evasiveness,
a snipe's lunatic forbearance.

Parchment damp, razor rusting,
I rehearse retreat to a beehive cell.

The world a dream of soft rain.
The sky a drizzle of angels.

Easter in Firle Park

It was an Easter of birds:
sparrows at their brawl and bicker,
a thrush on her garden nest,
the first chiffchaff's monotony.

In Firle Park high above the lake
young herons practised patience.
Freed from breeding, adults cavorted,
tumbling down the sky with titbits.

We sat on a plastic anorak,
mother and son, a generation.
You were planning to move house,
your final move. You wanted only

a few things around, photos,
a television, some furniture.
The grandchildren I don't provide.
Geese busybodied, martins purled

and laced the bright air. At home
we squabbled over the washing-up
like lovers. Chastened, we recoiled,

the girl shocked from your eyes,
our thoughts frozen as the stone peacock
we coveted outside the loggia.

Father

I'm trying on your collar,
a circlet of white bone.

I'm Robin Whitebreast,
a whistling in your skin.

You're coming clear in me,
a five o'clock shadow

at noon. Blackmailer,
coalface, you're in my neck

of the woods, your hands
collar my opened throat.

Yellow and Blue

It was yellow all the way
coming down from the monastery:
euphorbia's sulphur,
hellebore's greengold,
amber beads of fennel,
canary swags of broom,
dusty mustards of flax.

A butterfly escaped
from my father's collection,
a swallowtail resurrected
from those thin drawers,
where bodies of air
impaled on rusting pins
lifted threadbare wings.

A ruined tower released
a trickle of goats.
Brass bells splashed
and splintered over
the sun-conjured afternoon.

And then it was blue,
an iris by a pool,
chicory, gentian, comfrey,
the Spanish town drowning
in dusky seashadows,
swallows like thorns
breaking off the bush
of night, like weed
in the wind's tide.

When I was a child
my father said goodnight
to me in every language
he knew. When I heard
the Spanish words again
it was like finding a bird
ringed by his dead hands.

Harvest

Ancient tribute to fecundity
the harvest show flaunts its trophies.

Stranded on clean butcher's paper
dropsical marrows, ghost fans of wheat

and interminable carrots
trumpet the smug soil's virtue.

At a quiet hoop-la stall
the oldest lady I've ever seen

still plies her trade, in a dress
as faded as a Boer War battle flag.

Few children come to her stall
and they wander away, disconcerted

by the terrible determination with which
she moves through her darkness

to collect the hoops, sensing
somehow that they've missed the target.

Sitting, her vague bewildered eyes
search the air, as if it were

full of blows she must avoid.
Death is shadow-boxing with her.

She should have been gathered in long ago.
The routine of the stall is all

that's holding her here now.
Were she once to forget her lines

she would float away, light
and delicate as dandelion seed,

high over apples, beasts and children
into a silent, uncluttered barn.

Soap

On the bathroom sill
our dish of soaps:
jasmine, cucumber, rose.
Gifts, treats, sweet
necessities.

Puritan carbolic,
voluptuous Gallet,
palmolive for pilgrim.
For the jaded Caesar
imperial leather.

My favourite
was cocoa butter.
I kept the empty box
for years, its scent
a chink in time.

Think of it, lawyers
strewing rue across
the floor of chancery
to mask the stench
of poverty;

your grandmother,
goosegreased, sewn
into a vest for winter;
Great War soldiers
crunching lice.

Imagine the soaps
of heaven: astringent
rosemary, healing
feverfew, gentle cubes
of redemption.

Firelight

I'd light the fire without meaning to,
I'd light it without noticing,
kindling and coal using my hands
to combust on the very warmest of days.

You in the light green chair, me
in the dark green, we'd sit, fire
flowering between us, its black nightgowns
slipping to the floor. Already

memorable, the coal we burn
re-deposited within us,
mine of ripeness, seam of grace.
Where unknown others sat before

and unknown others will again
we'd take our time. Fire privy
to our intimacies, fire privy
to the unspoken questions:

What is the price of seclusion?
What have we missed, being childless?
Its mild blast on our skin always
a reminder, a hint of a darkness

burnt into human skin in suburbs far
from an explosion. Mask of Hiroshima,
shadow scorched into all our flesh.
Good servant, bad master, fire insists.

Last thing we'd lie awake and watch
dying flames infiltrate the bedroom
and dapple the walls. We'd hear
the soft toc as clinker hit the pan.

A sudden flare might send me stumbling
to check all was well. I'd hurry back,
sobered, in violation
of a privacy. To see the fire gently

collapsing, talking to itself, heating
empty chairs, was to know what
the world would look like when
we're not there. Was to be thin air.

In the Choir Stall

The choir vestry smelt of fart
and polish. You could hide
in the cupboard but the smell

would find you. The cassocks
had sweat-yellowed armpits,
odd buttons, torn linings.

We hid them under starch white
surplices, thin tin medallions
on coloured strings. Shoes

and faces betrayed us. I was 10
when Miss Blackstone keeled over
dead at matins. They locked

her ancient body in the vestry
until an ambulance could come.
I found the key and slipped in,

circled this object both there
and not there, losing its heat
on the gritty carpet. Her shoes

protruded. I wanted to lift
the cloth over her face but
was afraid she would look, afraid

she would not. At evensong
the cry rose in my throat, my days,
like the hymns, numbered.

The Coroner

A corpse is an envelope.
He whips it open, rummages
for trinket of cyst or tumour.

He never catches the last thing
on your mind. He wants
the body's reason to quit,

its hidden need to drop
all you thought it stood for
and let thought perish.

No one leaves without
a certificate. Detective
of inadvertent departure,

he breaks and enters
with drill and power saw,
ignores frayed nerves

to stand immune in gumboots
among the echoes of fever,
the catacombs of cancer,

the stalled unstartable hearts.
He redeems nothing but will
offer an ersatz eternity.

Cheeks touched up, smile
stitched up, a weight
off your mind: you'll never

look so well, a picture
of health to hang in the air
as the credits roll.

Hair Piece

When reading you used
catch, twist, lick
a strand of hair.

You'd place it gently
in your ear, until
it grew quite cold.

A circuit was completed,
a bright halo which
left me in the dark.

Now you've had your hair
cut short, your hands
flutter like moths

at the lamp of your ear.
I've made a ring
of hair.

It's a betrothal.
Try it for size.
It binds you to nothing.

The Hen Ark

The horse broke your heart,
one day knocked you
unconscious, made your life

unbearable. You'd had
enough of animal husbandry
but in the uncovenanted grace

of this Indian summer
sun gilds hexagons of wire
on a homemade hen ark.

You busy with scraps, armfuls
of feathery straw, divining
differences between

our six pullets. Through
cluck and chirr one comb
raddles and swells. Tonight

you bring the first egg,
its shell naïve and flawless
as your smile. Later

we crack it on a cup:
two gold yolks
in a wedding gown of albumen.

from *Catching The Light* (1996)

Angel

An angel showed me its wing
in a field at the back of the house.
It was leathery inside, vein-knotted,
welted with stitchmarks and scars.
There were fleas in the feathers
which it made me catch and crush.
You could feel the shafts buried
deep in the skin, like great nails.

I smuggled food, ointment for the wings.
Perhaps my father wouldn't have minded:
it was too dangerous to ask. Everyone
said we'd be better off without them.
There was talk of showtrials, mass graves,
of the need to be rid of them forever.
Some had appeared on TV, denying
they could fly, confessing to sexual acts.

The angel said it had almost been caught.
'I sheltered in a church, but they refuse
to acknowledge us, they're striking us
from the record, saying we never existed.'
It stayed for a month, sleeping by day.
I got used to the silhouette,
like that of a giant owl or moth
beating through the woods at dusk.

At first I took the blame when things
began to disappear from the house.
When my father's watch went missing
he forced the truth out of me.

I remember ragged shadows on the ground,
reassuring hands on my shoulder, voices
telling me I'd done the right thing,
quiet orders given to the dogs;

how the angel stood there in the lights
and just before all hell broke loose
how it opened its mouth and sang,
small tongue oddly neat and clean.
And the awful beauty of that song,
how it seemed to have nothing
to do with anything, seemed even then
to have forgotten where it came from.

The Last Tiger in Piltown

Though he's lent his name to
a wide range of jungle products,
he hasn't had to hunt in years.
He's sticking to the road now,
walking to numb a cramp,
stopping for a paper at Anthony's
or a pint of milk at O'Keeffe's.

When they needed to claim
he was making a comeback
they'd film him on the prowl,
let him stalk and savage
what seemed to be a goat,
advertising slipped into
the skin-pattern, the undergrowth.

Worst thing was the breeding.
In the absence of a female
they tried all kinds of substitute.
Most burst when he got excited.
These days he's just not up
to it, has frequent headaches.

But every inch is photographed,
genetic coding's nearly cracked,
a decent imitation should be
widely available soon.

He can't remember himself
which bits are meant to be real.
This afternoon, negotiations
over the new winter skin.

Tomorrow, a French TV crew,
another offer to found a religion,
the old attempt to finish his memoirs.

Often he's not there at all.
Just the door open, radio on,
vibration of stripes in a chair.
That fuel-shock, shimmer of air
above slightly parting grass.

Wood

The nice man who asked me to help him find golf balls
nursed a purple driver under his mac. By day
Teds oiled their quiffs and cycle chains, at night
they set fire to the rowing boats. The lake was lined
with broken glass. I cut my foot down to the bone,
watched a toad swallow the bleb of flesh. It wasn't
very good in the dark dark wood, just like Noddy said.

My mother warned I'd get an accent, promised me
a tin foot next time. Too late. I was in. I had mates.
They mocked my muscles, smaller than sparrows' kneecaps,
but I was alright. My sister warned me Dogger's mother
had had five children since his dad went to jail.
That didn't seem to matter. Until I told Dogger.
Though he chased me all the way, I just made it home,
slamming the front door on him, thanking my lucky stars
until the letterbox began to belch dogshit and sticks.

I shouted for my father, left him to sort it out,
stumped off down the hall to my own tinny applause.

North Coast

You'd no time for Amble harbour's broken silvers,
that nitid jigsaw simmering beyond the houses,
rickety piers crosshatching the collapse and curl.

You'd eyes only for sea coal, the smooth tablets
among the stones. Their salty flare. Free fuel.
You were head down on a fifties winter day

hunting those nuggets, hoping no one was watching,
hating the ocean's cold charity, your own need.
As for the dolphin out in the bay, we could keep it,

and its promise of unconditional love, and the sign
advising just how not to love it back. You'd started
on the unemployed Geordies, how they were stripping

the suburbs of videos to fund their Spanish holidays,
how their mining ancestors beat up yours, farmworkers
who dared to break their strike. No surprise then

at Newton your blindness to the wind-shaved waves,
the castle's moth-eaten silhouette, the auguries
of knot and dunlin. You, you'd homed in again—

on the square of fishing cottages; bijou lovenests
now but once, you insisted, so far from anywhere
women must have stood at their windows in tears,

facing into a day of washing, children and no company,
and bound to endure such isolation forever.

Edgeways

Lift up the town, you'd find him hanging on,
part of the archive, an anchored afterthought.

Where most, to mark their point of departure,
leave on the quayside shoes or a bag, he fastened

a rope, one end to an ankle, the other
to a bollard, before taking the plunge.

Whether he intended to save his family
the torment of long searching for his body,

whether he just wanted for the first and last time
to draw attention to himself, is not known.

Whatever, he made no mistake, so lost
in his own life there seemed no way back,

no Samaritan line, no breadcrumb trail.
He's still there, under the town, in parenthesis:

who took politeness to an extreme,
or who finally got a word in edgeways.

The Census

'I don't care what you find,'
said the sergeant, handing us
the forms. 'Just don't
find me any more land.'

The level-crossing gate
hadn't opened in years.
Bolts had rusted solid.
One might wait forever.

Last night you dreamt about
the room again, the room
inside the room. 'Perhaps,'
you said, 'It dreamt about me.'

We found the train in a field.
Our great eyes filled up
the windows as we stared in
on the tiny frozen passengers.

You

We weren't sympathetic, were we?
Our lines were always engaged.
We don't hear much from you lately—
are you losing hope now we've aged?

You can still make your absence felt—
at the meal-table, too long a pause.
Pampered cats. Too neat a garden.
In such ways you plead your cause.

One time at least you came close,
by mistake, as they say it should be.
You must have thought this was it,
at last the passage was free.

You'd begun to head for the entrance,
we stood by, prepared to receive.
In the end it was all a mix-up,
and face it, we were relieved.

We're not half the people we should be.
Too lightly we walk on this earth.
Cowards, selfish, your voice whispers.
Be devils. Be parents. Give birth.

I'll stop your world from shrinking.
I'll save you from dying out.
I'll console the surviving partner—
it's got to be worth trying out.

No decision is final of course.
Believe me your hearing's been fair.
But it looks as if this is the verdict:
might have been but never were.

Don't hold your absence against us.
You have your place in the parade.
You'll be there forever between us,
a difference we never made.

The Silence Cloth

the silence cloth has been laid out
the table's neatly spread
we're using the best china cups
don't mention that he's dead

you've changed the car again I see
it's true what someone said
it's best to change them frequently
don't mention that he's dead

to see exactly what was there
they opened his brave head
do have another sandwich please
don't mention that he's dead

and you must be his brother's son
the one he knew as Fred
a close resemblance certainly
apart from the fact he's dead

isn't the garden lovely now
that's a lark overhead
I wonder why it sings so much
he can't sing he's dead

he's buried in the potting shed
he's buried in the bed
he's surely going to haunt us all
if we don't say he's dead

he's living in the larder
he's living in the head
he's living in the silence
of not being said to be dead

yes of course you must go now
goodness how time's fled
I'm going to close the door now
and never mention he's dead

Here

Members of the lesser religions call,
lost salesmen. It's rarely I can help.
Farmers pass by on their way to the bank,
tractors rejoicing every inch of the way.

To these rituals we attend: sugar beet trains
in autumn, the farmgate's one-note xylophone,
the polite applause of horseshoes on tarmac.
Herons haunt us. Even the stars look lost.

We don't know what we're doing here at all.
When your mother phones your voice reverts
to geordie, as if you'd never left, as if
we'd never met. There must be some mistake.

At night the fire takes photographs of us.
Film streams up the chimney, out into
the outside world, straight up to what
we used to know as heaven. Big deal.

It's the sound of geese flying overhead
makes you feel at home. Or was that homeless?

Breaking Ground

The digger was breaking an entrance into the garden,
busting down elder and hawthorn scrub, lobbing it
on to a green fire primed with tyres and petrol.
It was a cold summer night, dark and stormy.

Neighbours and I stood hunched in the smoking rain
to appraise the driver's precision. He could take
the tights off a lady with that small bucket;
he could part your hair. Delving into an old midden

each bucketful deserved archaeology. Bedsprings,
they could talk. That teapot could spout forth.
Leg, horse, marriage, record, our talk was all
of breaking until suddenly the digger drove

through and the garden exposed in its headlights
took the words clean out of our mouths. Beaten
down by rain, skulking in shrubs, light hugged
its own poor flesh, as if we had stumbled into

the heart of sorrow, where light must grieve
for every broken thing it shines upon here.
At such a clearing's edge we were trespassers,
only shadow to turn to, and the loss in words.

Main de Gloire

Cut the hand, left or right, from a felon's corpse
hanging on a roadside gibbet. Wrap in winding sheet.
Squeeze tight as possible to drive out any last blood.
For two weeks let it seethe with nitre, salt,
zimort and long peppers, in an earthenware retort.
Dry in an oven heated by fern and vervain.
In the dog days expose to the sun.

Make a candle from virgin wax, Sisamie de Laponie
and a hanged man's fat. Thrust between the fingers
of the hand and light, or use the hand itself,
lighting the thumb and all the fingers.
Now you may steal with impunity: the flame
will prevent sleepers from waking
and stupefy anyone you show it to.

It cannot be blown out by any ordinary person,
nor be extinguished by any liquid save milk.
If the thumb does not catch, beware: someone
is still awake, or unaffected. Do not use where
a threshold is smeared with a black cat's gall,
a white hen's liver or a screech owl's blood. Nor
where there is a large dog, or a burglar alarm.

Palm

after Rilke

Old sole you've gone soft—
too much walking on air.

Sole which on feeling now
learns with feeling to tread.

Meadow of my hand, meadow
which finds other meadows,

makes with them landscape,
filled with meeting.

Palm, calm troubled bed
deep-creased by longing.

Inner shell shaped
to a fruit formed in prayer.

Broken home of wholeness,
by the faraway stars

orphaned and enchanted.

Red-Handed

In the darkness of the church
I felt more than saw. Troubled
shadow. Air scratching itself:
a small bird, locked in.

I opened the main door wide.
A bale of warm air fell in,
a cartoon invitation, spiced
with seed and faint sound.

The bird wouldn't buy it.
Over it flew and over against
the sealed chancel windows.
I'd never catch it and yet,

out of its element, estranged,
it seemed somehow we had met.
At length it lay down on
a limestone sill, staring up

at me, resigned. Entreaty
nerved the air between us.
I would carry it down, let it
go into the bright afternoon.

It wouldn't let me touch.
Always at the last moment flew.
There are no safe hands, all
have tasted money, or blood.

Herons

1

Water stalker, river's eyelash,
when you descended to my pool

you made a fool of yourself,
daft as any god in close-up,

twitchy, verminous, uncertain,
out of true in the domestic,

shooed away. Tangled puppet
you gangled up, a squirt

of fishy piss your final word,
open to any interpretation.

Keep that distance now.
Let your far cry bring

jungle to farmland,
prehistory to present.

Be willow by water, be needle
to thread the edges

of sight, seaming those edges
like appetite, prayer.

2

Herons were always here. The one we saw
on the day we moved in seemed an omen.
We named the house for it, wanted
Beware of the Heron painted on the gate.

One gangled often up into the air
off the dyke opposite, a sack of sticks,
almost forgetting its legs, doomed
to crash but finding grace with distance.

Gods need distance. This one stumbled up
from that dyke with one wing pointing
the wrong way. Tried to fly. Fell. Ran
across the field like a frightened child.

For days it skulked in the waterways,
one step ahead of the fox, wing upraised
to ward off the enormous rebuke of sky,
the brightness it had fallen from.

It drew blood when the wildlife ranger
trapped it, folding its gorgeous plumage
in a blanket. He re-broke the wing, set it.
It could have flown, but wouldn't. Starved.

To the ground we returned the standstill
of wing, the stained glass eye, the closed
vowel of stomach. The silence of cry.
All the dried ingredients of grace.

Halcyon

I've never seen the kingfisher
you claim to have witnessed
on the stand of brackish water
at the edge of our wood.

Years I've been looking.
Not a sign. Wrong habitat
too: no bank for nesting,
indeed no fish. Face it

there was no bird, yet
each time I pass I peer into
that gloom and each time
this comes to mind:

a flash of chestnutsapphire.
A small flame brooding on ooze.
Your words made light.
Your bright idea. You diving

through the long years
of grief to surface here,
halcyon, incorruptible.
And not one bird but a pair.

November

Overnight the sycamore collapses,
leaves black-blistered, cracking into scraps.
The lime tree takes its time, yellows flaming
gently through a pebble lens of mist.

Lifting a stone loose from a wall I find
a mass of snail shells, all empty.
Fieldfares racket over after berries.
Gunfire disappears down its own echo.

Across the river, geese are drifting down
to print the inches. Rolled pellets, a wisp
of down, flattened grass are all we can find.
We might be our own ghosts, returning.

Butter of leaves at its feet, the lime stands
astonished, holding nothing up to nothing.

Marsh Marigolds

The leaves go unnoticed most of the year
but chance to glance down in March
you'll see these fat buttery suns glow
in the darkness of dykes like the headlights
of a dense green traffic streaming south.

Carlicups, downscombs, bluddas, Johnny cranes,
they go under more than a hundred names
but little do they care as they brighten
like buttons on the suit of a golden giant
asleep in the soft black mud under alders.

Appetite

The goldfish was basking side-on in the sun,
a fleck of blood in the pond's brown lens.

When it moved I saw pincered inches:
four black beetles, locked on.

Hungry surgeons, their knives went deep.
White flesh shone against the dark shells.

Mouthing Os of despair, its glamorous face
not framed for pain, the fish was still breathing.

All caught in a net, held up in the air,
the spectacle continued, the beetles feasting,

the fish gasping, until I killed them all.
Even now I can feel those jaws working.

No Problem

It had started when we kept the fires lit
all summer, though we didn't know it then.
July lanes blackened by coal lorries
were just something else to moan about.

Winter snow was novel, a good excuse
not to go to work. Sleds were made,
rusted iceskates brought down, new markets
created for thermal jackets, exotic headgear.

When did we first notice that the snow
stayed on the mountains all year round?
That plants were moving down, cloudberry
and three-leaved rush common in the meadows?

When a penguin was seen in Donegal
it just seemed a freak; when more came next year
we felt strangely honoured, singled out.
A special set of stamps was printed.

We soon got used to the icebergs offshore,
the glassy rim thickening beyond the beaches.
Bets are being taken on the chances
of walking across to the neighbouring island,

which still enjoys sunshine we believe.
Some brave souls have skated off already,
hissing into the dark. As yet they've sent
no word, but we know they won't forget us.

They say some areas are cut off completely.
The TV shows only white static, as if somehow
it were speaking on behalf of the cold.
Good will come of it, of that we're certain.

The Sun Room

Six foot of hardcore stood between us and damp
when we moved in, but the dark wouldn't budge.
Even after we'd cleared the sills of relics, windows
seemed hostile to light, loath to give it floorspace.

So we broached the endwall, built a glass room,
a great wound of light which reached into every corner.
And all summer we were home and dry, photocopied
by the kind sun, but in autumn our breath began

to fog the glass, dripping back down onto our food.
Now the steady blade of a dehumidifier bales up
every drop of moisture. I wait for the red light
to announce it's full, waiting to collect each

liquid ingot, each bright pint full of us.
Could they reconstruct our lives from these—
our shining, inconsequential archives? I carry
the container to the sink, start to pour, Moses

woken from a bad dream, arms full of water and light.

Letter from Ladakh

Nights are so long without you
though I hold heaven in my arms
in a silence that reaches to Russia.

Learning the art of non-attachment
proves hard. It is good to share
my life with you: distance seems
to make us closer and who's to say
now where I end, where you begin?

Truth is if I cannot sleep with you
I cannot sleep without you, so I lie
awake, rehearsing what I've seen:
white thistles in a downpour of light,
old cans used to protect the trunks
of young trees, the way night
folds away mountains to disclose
the simple, kind machinery of stars.

Everything's alright then, so it seems,
but the meditation's a dead loss.
I can't sit in the right position,
my back's killing me, I can't concentrate,
can't stop relating all this to you.

Water's always looking for the quickest
way out of this high and dry land.
Its sound seems to sharpen the silence.
That's how I've seen our attachment:
sound as the ring on a finger of silence.

'You went a long way to find that out,'
I hear you say. I know, fine words butter
no parsnips, you didn't come up the Tyne
on a bike. 'Far be it from me to demur,'
I'm muttering aloud, in that smarmy way
I think I know you love to hate.

Catching the Light

Over Gortrush Wood, low on the horizon,
an orange husk of moon.
One star burning in the last wash of sunlight
higher in the sky.
All still but for the hum of a generator,
odd twang of a snipe.

Soil sleeps on its bed of rock. Moths might be
flakes of wood
on the housewall. Skins of dark form
over skins of dark
and all are caught in my net of sight,
both me and what I see.

Medusas, my eyes: what they say they see
my tongue has no choice
but to confirm. No slipping the tongue.
No such thing as no idea.
Moon. Wood. Horizon. Habits of a lifetime,
words made flesh

but what seems to lie beyond them tonight seems
not emptiness but
light, or what we call light. Not to be grasped,
not to be spilt.
Moon. Wood. Horizon. Made of light.
Moth, snipe: light.

In a world of light we are creatures of distinction
lost and found
as we speak. Lost and found at this given moment

in the wonder of saying
an orange husk of moon low on the horizon
over Gortrush Wood.

Unbecoming

For too long he has stood at your door,
this small bewildered boy, fringe hung
over national-health specked eyes,
timbertongued boy, unworthy of mention.

For too long in his only mirror,
your eye, he has seen himself
othered, ambered, pupilled, only meal
in that eye's desert his own tears.

It is time to let him in. Time
to sit him down and serve him.
Take off your arms. Take out your eyes.
Enter his mouth. Loosen his tongue.

Listen. All his life he has loved you.
Take his word. Onto his heart graft your heart.

Prayer

How we survive, Lord. Twenty-two homes,
sixteen schools before we were ten.
Those blind uncles touching us up.
Our wounds wide open, our words not heard
until we wept, but were not allowed to.
O the tears uncried strained against
the eyes, the good conduct medals.

It's no wonder, Lord. Fingers at
the underwear, fists in the stomach,
stories spooled inside us, pleading
to be repeated. Look at us, crawling
from the wrecks of our childhoods,
begging any stranger for a hug.
O what happened. And what happened.

Let us praise, tonight, ourselves.
Our flesh, bones, eyes, hands, hair.
The brightness of our being.
How should our light not shine?
Look at us, Lord, praise us,
real tonight as each other,
as real as can be. Beyond belief
our beauty, our right to be here.

What the Deer Said

I am my shyness, said the deer.
I am not searching for common ground.
I do not need to be cured.

What makes me tremble so?
The world's infinite sweetness,
sweetness by fear ripened.

Not our song but our silence
passes all understanding.
And we are silent when we sing.

If love can be a measure of distance
grant me that distance.
I am my shyness. Love my shyness.

Scythe

Come with me into the barn.
Feel, first, the cold space, how
it enters into wall and floor

and how this cold space humbles,
peels away stock feeling
to leave you in a new place.

Take the scythe down from its hook.
Weigh the strange trembly blade,
know it finds poise only in motion.

Take it outside, into the darkness.
Brace yourself. So. Start to swing.
Imagine: you are reaping silence.

Bright sheaves of silence.
With each swing watch them fall.
Work hard to keep the rhythm, work

until the scythe swings itself.
Now look back. Find those sheaves
not fallen at all but sprung

again, unbroken, multiplying
and you the reaper cutting
your way to the field's core.

Do not look for absolutes.
You will hear many small noises,
you will hear your own blood—

should you hear a bird call
understand it as a finger
on the lips of silence.

Work until you are being worked,
until there is only you and the scythe,
until there is neither you nor scythe

until there is only what there is.

from *Whereabouts* (2005)

Swallow

A spent firework
on the lawn.

Tiny feet still
hooked on space.

Wings wind-sleek,
head sleek with wind.

So full of flight
it must have died

of ripeness.
In the tail's V

a stalk of sky.

Him

So many people claim to know him well.
They tell you stories which make perfect sense.
These are his habits. His hobbies. His friends.
Address? Photo? Belongings? Look. Right here.

Of course it wasn't always plain sailing.
It appears that X led to Y. That if
he'd only done A instead of B,
C couldn't possibly have happened.

There was something unique about him.
It was his way of talking. His silence.
The way he did whatever he did. Etcetera.
You'd know when you'd been in his company.

When this stranger claims, as he will, to be
your self, on no account believe him.
Dates, names, events, will coincide. The rest
is made up. You know it wasn't like that.

Send him on his way with a good thrashing.
Let the moon and stars weigh down your tongue.
Envy their solitudes. Do not pretend
you are anything other than lonely.

Woodpecker

You come home and tell me you've seen,
for the first time, a woodpecker,
feeding at the coconut shell
hung in your brother-in-law's tree.

What kind was it I want to know.
There are 3 kinds, black, green, spotted.
One laughs, it's known as a yaffle.
There aren't any in Ireland.

You can't remember its colour.
It flew slowly down to the tree,
edged its way out towards the shell,
began to eat, you can see it now

and you shape it in the air for me,
one hand carefully cupping
the weight of what it meant,
you hold it there for me as if

I'd never broken anything
you'd ever given me and it starts
to cross the space between us
and I do not know what to say.

Skip

At the end of a long night you drive home
to the house you know is empty, but warm.
You'll let yourself relax, doze by the fire.
Just one stop to make on the way home,
to chuck the rubbish into a factory skip.
You drive quietly into the car park:
the lights are still on in the factory,
you know you're not supposed to use their skip.
Unlock the boot, heave the bag up and away.
Get back in to start the car—find you've no keys.
Realize you've chucked them away with the bag,
into twelve deep feet of tangled rubbish.
You can't ask the factory men for help.
There's no one at home and you're miles from it.
You sit in the car. Misled by a streetlamp
into thinking it's day, a bird starts to sing.
You open the window to hear it better.
It's the robin, you seem to remember,
gets fooled like that. Or is it the chaffinch?

The Toy Museum

Glassed in at the turn of the stairs
leading up to the Toy Museum,
all shapes and sizes, some patched,
others good as new, they're all seated,
all staring straight ahead.

And all have their arms outstretched,
as if their children had just left,
as if at any moment those children,
the Bonzoes and the Bunties,
the Jimjams, the Jenjens, might return,

as if time and flesh could be rewound
and they could all come streaming back,
out of the earth and out of the fire,
through white hair, wounds, weddings,
into suits of innocence, this embrace.

And no one can tell the bears how
the years add themselves to the years,
how children go raining into the dark.
Love blazing off their golden coats,
absence burning in their arms, they stare on.

Home

Goodbye you had to say to every room
when as a child you went out—those rooms
might not be there when you returned.

Even now, when you've been out, you like
to creep back and stare through your windows—
as if to catch the rooms by surprise.

To see what they look like in your absence.
Or to snatch a glimpse of yourself—the house
a mirror which might make that self seem true.

It's you, you, the one that lives here, you want
it to say; the more you look the harder
you are to find. You see books on shelves,

spoons in drawers, everything in its right place—
but you know they're not talking about you.
They forget you as soon as you leave.

You stare into your reflection, trapped
inside the glass, neither here nor there.
A stranger always you were, you will be.

And This is True

And this is true too, a young fox ambling
through pink campion, bluebell, ramson
on a spring evening.

Despite everything, what's been, what will come,
the violence, the murder, the terrible news,
a vivid burn of fur,

a beautiful face, are also true. Dare you say
it seems not to have a care in the world?
It seems not to.

You're making this up of course: the fox
walks in a trace of your making, your eyes
impose this pattern.

And it's no more true than the heavy fox
you dragged off the road by its tail,
its face a smashed fruit.

No more true than the fox breaking into
the henhouse, tearing all the heads
off all the chickens.

Than what your country did to others.
Than the buried children. Than hunger. Than all
you have to answer for,

than all those with neither time nor freedom
to stop to watch a fox in thick flower
amble towards them.

And there are so many. And it's true
the fox will see you, turn and run,
eyes full of fear.

Now it ambles towards you, through campion,
bluebell, ramson, on a spring evening.
Do not doubt it.

Sleeping with the Kingfisher

Its appearance in the bed wasn't surprising.
Giraldus said a dead one kept linen fresh.

No, what surprised was the size of the thing
and the way it hugged me close to its breast.

To feel its bill run the rule down my spine.
To be enfolded in sapphire wings. Surprising.

How much more so to wake and find myself ablaze,
my heart the blue seed in a blossom of flame.

The Inner Poet

Hi, it's me. Yes, I know
this is an awkward time.
And it's getting longer
the more you listen to me.

I know you're up there
in front of an audience
hoping to look calm,
trying to look inspired.

That's why I'm here in fact.
I'd like to help. Let's start
with an old reminder.
One from the childhood.

Carol concert, wasn't it?
You were picked to sing solo.
Only picked because
your dad was the vicar.

You started the show.
But your voice wouldn't
do what you wanted it to.
You sounded like a fool.

Remember how everyone
stared at you? Course you do.
How you cried? Bad,
wasn't it, bad as could be.

You often say you'll never
get over that moment.
You're probably right.
Gottago. Have a good one.

The First Move

When the grids you slot them into dissolve,
think how people always surprise you.
Always better, kinder, than you allowed.
Think how each suffers as much and more than you.

Think how you love the things of this world.
The birds, the stone, the flowers, the water.
Everything that cannot love you back.
How easy to love the wordless wild and dead.

Your father said he believed in mercy,
not forgiveness. You never forgave him.
Think how the heart hardens in its cage,
repeating its moves. You must learn how to love.

Digestion

Since it all comes down to digestion,
one thing's growth another thing's decay,
it's just as well those bitter juices
do their job unseen, just as well
that animals crawl into the dark to die,
just as well the ground makes such short work.
Thank the thoughtful eye for the way
it looks to heal this breaking world,
and since one thing so quickly becomes
another, learn to cherish examples
of the most gentle digestion:
the suede shoe stood on its own so long
in a field, sole being parted
with such infinite care from upper;
or, in that monastery crypt, the way
the tomb of a monk buried in a wall
has opened, and a spotlight picks out
his old bones: a dark crumble of honey.

Red Admirals

Of the reddened leaves
drifting to earth
three or four seem
jerked into life,

soft, erratic flames
wandering on wings
too gorgeous for gravity.

Drunk on windfall
they settle
on a white wall,

bloody fingerprints,
small fires
on the edge of night.

The world wheels
under pitiless stars
into dark—

after such dark
what colour
can there be?

A robin's dull ember
in the wreck
of a tree.

Entries

Falcons, we thought. Blunt tails and curved wings
fooled us as the birds swung across a distant cliff.

Swifts we knew them for close-up: alpine swifts,
riding on the updraughts off the limestone,

breasts half-mooned as if rubbed clean
by the light and heat beating off water and stone.

We watched them until they flew inside us.
Though we'll forget them they'll never leave,

flying at the mention of their name,
coming at odd intervals unbidden.

Not just as remembered but part now
of what remembers them. Entered also

by the light of our watching them together.

The Home Fire

Saturday dusks, Eddie Waring warbling on
before the wrestling, then the football results,
magical names, Hotspur to Hamilton Academicals.

The smell of new mud from boots drying by the fire,
its tile surround adorned by biblical scenes,
the jawbone of an ass, that hairy man Esau,

and the fire heaped with tarblocks that crackled
and spat so much they turned us all into goalies,
diving around to extinguish smouldering carpet.

Fighting later for a place on the leather sofa
whose brass studs could make you see stars,
and one night allowed to stay up late to watch

Johanssen fight Patterson, live, our reflections
and the fireglow dancing in the small screen,
all of us there, in and out of the glass.

Then the long trek to bed, across the cold flags
of the hall, ice of air shaken by a huge clock's
erratic tick, shadows thick with menace.

Up the stairs, never touching the two iron rungs
in the wooden bannister, running past the ghost
at the turn of the steps, across the landing

and safe into bed, just to lie there,
cradled by the rhythms of the Northern trains,
watching headlights polish the ceiling. Waking

to hear doves crooning, sunlight at the curtains
with a sack of golden air; waking to find
the room gone, adults gone, fire out, roof off,

darkness and stars raining down on my bared head.

Saturday Morning

Saturday morning, tea in the pot,
cats on a quilt worn past repair.

Outside the window, the low hills,
stony light, horses in Kearns's field.

Old dried leaf, fresh water. Given cups.
Dust motes in steam. Touch of known skin.

Skin that we're shy of all over again.
That we try to hide from each other.

Which sags, has wrinkles, is mottled.
From which things need to be cut out.

Bodies once so well known to us,
now unknown. Which let us down.

Bodies we're ashamed of, angry about,
find difficult to accept as ours.

Which are no longer possessed
but possess us, at times disgust.

Not the bodies we fell in love with,
couldn't wait to undress.

This was happening all the time
behind the screens of desire.

Bodies grown old and tired, needing
more than ever now to be loved.

Bodies which have grown into each other,
which if separated might not survive.

Tea in the pot. Old dried leaf, fresh water.
Given cups. Us two, in deep.

For All You Know

For all you know
you might need the eye
of the little egret

bent on these fields,
a refuge from storm,
for the first time.

Assume its reception
above the hedged lanes,
the drowning river.

Let its yellow toe
root in corners,
queer the pitch.

Bring its black beak
to bear on the pane
of the flood-puddle:

to muddy the water,
to cloud the issue
for all you know.

Starling

Starlings join to make one single-minded machine.
Whatever tree they land on
becomes a starling tree.

Above the railway line great flocks flow from shape to shape,
black lakes which flatten, tilt,
stretch, turn over, fold.

It would appear they cannot bear to be parted.
Tonight one gone astray
divebombs the bird table.

A nosey, nasty crowd of one, soon it's driven
all the other birds away.
No more come. Then what?

It shoots across the garden, jabs its unchoired beak
into the bird box.
No one there. So now?

Twitches. Looks around. Looks out across the fields.
All the unconverted air.
The horrid unblack blue.

Takes off its coat. Why not? Unfastens beak and bone.
Loses sight of itself.
Starts a new life. Alone.

Leaf

Pontevedra, August '96, it reads,
this dried leaf picked up in a park,
inscribed, kept for a bookmark.

Taken for granted now, colour faded,
fabric starting to tatter, leafliness
so lost in function it comes

as a shock to see, accidentally held
against bright sun, how the leaf
turns into an x-ray of itself.

Such intricate veining and staining.
Such detailed, unknowable history.
Such private life, such suchness

in this leaf, held in this hand,
in this field of sunlight and shadow.
At this moment. In this hand.

Leaf of the hand, leaf of touch.
Leaf of light, of air, leaf of sight.
Leaf of emptiness, leaf of form.

Face

When boiling soup splashed up
to scald your cheek, that was
one shock. When people moved
to avoid your bandaged glare
in a bar, that was another.
Face changed, you were changed.

As a child I wondered which face
I would wear in heaven: my then face,
my adult one, my old age one?
And what about parents, friends?
Which ones would they be wearing?
How would anyone be recognized?

Faces won't matter, I was told.
Spirits don't have them.
Even then I suspected no one
could exist without flesh:
face, spirit, were not separate
nor would either be saved.

On the tiny field of new skin
around your eye, a soft gold down
grows again. When you're cold
or tired, the slight scar darkens:
as if death had held you, admired,
left a fingerprint, a maker's mark.

Rain

This freckle
of rain on the roof,
it's the gentlest siege,
not wanting
to come in, nor disturb
our sleep, seeming
to lose interest, fading,
then coming back,
a quiet insistence,
someone touching
unexpectedly
your arm as they speak,
the faintest of faint
invitations
to follow, to spread
out over broken
oak leaves,
over purple stones
and sleeping birds,
to lose face,
be dispersed.

Need

All day I've tidied you away:
the bath's ghost of scented steam,
a tap's dye ring, your weight from cushions,
your shape from the bed.

All day I've worn your presence away
as if hunting some seamless silence
out of which you can't be shaken,
some place where you might survive
with no outward or visible sign.

At night, when silence won't answer back,
in the mirror I see the boy trained
not to cry, taught mercy not forgiveness,
who must not show his hurt,
who must prove he can do without you.

All day I've tidied his need away.

Career

The boy lies full-length
on a green-painted pew
in a corner of the garden,

one hand on a stick
nailed into its wood,
the control for this rocket

from whose window shrink
the voices and faces
of those who love him,

the anxious concern,
the expectation,
the chart of his course.

Now he can take it all in:
the circuits of amber
that night makes of cities,

the poster-paint fields,
the soft nose of land
dipped in a saucer of sea;

now he is weightless,
a space in which these things
can see themselves.

He lets go of the stick,
disconnects his mike.
The calls for re-entry

will not get through.
From such a career
how should he return,

to be known again,
to be the boy
his family think he is;

how forget all this space;
how fit himself
back into his face?

The Broken Fields

Driving home through the dark
an owl slides past the windscreen.

Fearing I might have hit it
I stop, get out to look—
only an old paper bag.

Only a grieving wind.
Only fields stretching away,
broken fields, aching
in their chemical chains.

Van Gogh's 'The Farm'

Where does it come from, this farm
and the light which wraps this farm
in sage blessing, light of welcome return?

When it was never my life to cross a field
at dusk, to open a blue door, to know
the squeak of its latch and the way

it's being listened for with love,
why should it all seem so familiar?
Why second nature to take water from a water-sweated jug,

to know each stair's creak, to feel worn sheets
roughly cool my skin, to watch shadows
house and unhouse the sloped ceiling?

Look at those figures crossing the yard,
how their lives seem to have shaped them
to their own shapes, shapes intended:

they travel in air that fits them, through light
that loves them, in joined and finished life.
They will always know where they are going.

Peck

After six years of living as a pair
one hen sickened, hunched up, as if
trying to climb back inside herself.
The other bird stood over her, on guard,
fussing, attentive, concerned, it seemed.
Close-up I could see she was pecking,
pulling out feathers around the neck
of the sick bird, baring flesh to eat.

I shouldn't have been surprised.
Everything lives off something else.
Flesh, bones, rocks, soil, selves, days,
what can they be made of but lives?
What's the great sun in all its glory
but a lustrous hen, pecking us, itself, away?

The Robin

For days it kept on tapping at the window,
a spent coal trying to regain a fire,
a little glowing boat beating against
a wall of surf, a frozen sheet of spray.

When we opened the window, in it flew.
Began, it seemed, to search, as if for what
had been there when it was out, but now
was out when it was in. Soon it was tapping

at the window again, from the inside, as if
the real thing was to cross that barrier,
as if the real world lay beyond
and it were living in a realm of shadow.

When you read it was after its reflection,
thinking it a rival, or a partner,
we saw that image growing in its head,
an ideal bird in an ideal space, we saw

the little robin storm the gates of heaven
and find itself bewildered and alone,
finding that heavens depend upon not
being entered, there being no other side.

We might have seen it homeless then, flying
back into a world suddenly strange,
provisional, a stage set to be ransacked
for hints of another, better place—

but it flew straight into its world, its home,
straight into its struggle and its song.
In the window, looking on, we saw ourselves:
in our minds that glass, that image entered.

Swan House

1

And what were we to make of that swan
which came crashing through the mist, low
over the house like a lost glory,
so sudden it was gone before it came,
re-assumed into mist, its light
only seeming to reach us then, as if
we only saw it when we breathed the word *Swan*,
as if all recognition were farewell.

2

Slower than sound but faster than words
it came, an echo preceding its source,
the mist rhythmed, strained to breaking
until sound was above us, the air
hallowed by steady magnificent applause
which drew us up and in until
we both were, and were received into,
the house of our astonished praise.

Magwitch

If I went out in a peasouper fog
I'd have to wear a hankie over my mouth.

Later, where my mouth had been, I'd find
a dark stain, in the shape of a kiss.

Out there, lost at first, I'd learnt
to find my way from one lamppost to the next.

It all seemed crazy in daylight. Crazy
how one night Magwitch followed me

out of the TV into the fog, crazy
how his hand reached to clutch my ankle.

If I lifted my hankie, if I didn't cry out,
was it because I knew, even then,

I'd sooner breathe poison
than risk betrayal of that hand?

Father on whose love I choke, love me.

Snipe

That small heart
plunged through our own.

All over the sky
these scars of sound,
this listening.

Where we could
never be,
but were.

Elder

I come home these nights under such light,
alleys of softly glowing elder
in whose flower the bridal whites discolour,
spring freshness sours into summer.

Rubbledrudge, thicketskivvy, your mild moons
wax where they're left, part of the undergrowth,
swagged with bramble, woodbine, taken for granted
and only too content to leave it that way.

Elder, if you shy away from these words
who could blame you? Ancient hatreds
haunt and hover like clouds of summer flies.
God's stinking tree, you had much to answer for.

On your wood Christ was crucified, Judas hanged.
Boats made of elder sunk, cradles sickened.
The hand of a man struck with elder sprouted
from its grave. What did you do wrong?

Perhaps it was your hazy status. Neither bush
nor tree. Never straight nor strong. Stems thick
but hollow. Scent half-piss, half-champagne.
Such uncertainty could only mean one thing.

How have you answered our thought's poison?
Found the common ground. Bent your back.
Fed the winter thrush with your berries.
Spun these discs of chalky clotted light.

Asked nothing. Asked only to be what you are.
Not like anything. Not like anything at all.

Harriers

You might see a marsh harrier, the warden said.
But that's all. Wrong season. Worst time of day.

We walked to the tower, through fierce noon heat.
Climbed up. Stood. Stared. At nothing. All we saw
was that marsh harrier, once, in the distance.

"If we hurry," you said, "we might just catch
the ten-to-four bus." "We'll never make it,"
I said, "it's gone 2." "So what do you suggest?"
"There's a way back through the reeds,
look here on the map." "That'll take hours—
we've no food, no water." "Have it your way."
"No, we'll try the reeds." "No, I don't want to."

Half running back, through still fierce heat,
hating ourselves as much as each other,
checking watches again and again, we just
made the bus, fell straight into hysterical sleep,
jerking awake, sweat spitting out of our heads.

Behind us, the reedbeds. The huge sky.
The green canal. Yellow waterlilies.
Emptiness. The ten thousand things.

Heron

Every now and then, often at dusk,
as if to darken the darkness of dark,

over the house a heron wrings out
its terrible cry: a note, long pondered,

exactly the same as all preceding, all
to come, to add to that lifelong solo

whose scale, slowness, lack of closure,
whose unchanging survey and sum of sorrow

and sadness and sadness and sorrow,
whose utter lack of meaning and hope

make even the most heart-rending lament
seem child's play, merest self-pity.

Whereabouts

Take the road under
the twisting oaks
when the mountain turns
so blue you think
you can see through it.

Beside the bridge
winter heliotrope,
a visitor from India,
sets out its stall.
Mimulus from China
spills its seed
on the stream.

Two stone piers
astray in a field—
on which side
was the way in?

A blackbird's slither
and scald,
a wren's rattle.

The beat of my heart
going, in the silence,
its own way.

～

Crooked gorse—
on its sleeve
one too many
hearts of gold.

～

A burnt log,
a Snowcream carton,
evergreen branches,
flattened verge rising:
no camp continues.

～

Whose are they,
eyes, hands, voice,
the thoughts that build,
the thoughts that build?

～

On a breeze
the ghost of snipe,
of woodcock
enough and to spare.

～

Drained obedient fields,
water's tame trickle
through concrete pipes.
Overhead a satellite
counts the cows.

&

Miraculous wound,
the roses that still flower
where a house once was.

&

In the horse's eye,
nothing rests.

&

Ballyglassoon, Dowlin,
Tobernafauna, Cahill's Hill.

&

Over the tall grass
swallows dip and dive,
one minute here,
the next gone.

&

Limestone, lichen,
dandelion, cloud, all
in their own good time.

&

New bungalows rising
out of the ground
overnight, ivy
stripped off
the old demesne wall.

≈

A heron's cry,
sileage bales
like gorged torsos.

≈

The fields that run
through my head
are still the fields,
sodden after rain.

≈

Cow parsley holds
a ruined head to sun—
a saint, nicotine brown,
smoked to the butt by God.

≈

Whose life turns out
the way they meant it to?
Who knows whose turn
it is to die?

≈

Fruit at its feet
the crab tree implores,
beggar who knows it wiser
to give than receive.

≈

Look back the way
you came: the more
you look the less
it leads to you.

≈

By the No Dumping sign
a fridge, some shoes,
two armchairs.
In the dyke
a dead pig.

≈

A squashed crow's wing
lifts and waves
in the wake of a passing car.

≈

How deeply
everything forgets
I was ever here.

≈

Butterfly orchids,
fifteen this year
in Tom Quinn's field.

❧

Love for these things
becomes the prayer
you offer to all
that is not thing.

❧

A ram's horn
on the grass,
a comma linking
future to past.

❧

A wind you can't see
roughs to silver
first one patch of grass,
then another.

Printed in the United Kingdom
by Lightning Source UK Ltd.
133183UK00001B/151-168/P